EYES ON FIRE

Witnesses to the Detroit Riots of 1967

2nd Edition

Edited by

HEATHER BUCHANAN SHARON STANFORD

TERESA KIMBLE

AQUARIUS PRESS
Detroit, MI

Eyes on Fire: Witnesses to the Detroit Riots of 1967
2nd Edition

Editors: Heather Buchanan, Sharon Stanford and Teresa Kimball
Cover art: Aquarius Press LLC

ISBN 978-0-9718214-8-4

AQUARIUS PRESS
www.AquariusPress.net

Contents

PREFACE

Why did it happen? As with so many other major urban riots/rebellions, it is hard to pinpoint the exact moment, the moment when the atmosphere became charged, electrifying and scorching everyone in sight. I believe that witnesses to the Detroit Riots of 1967 are still filtering and processing those five days of fire in their city, their home. Some people do not wish to remember, but most cannot forget and have held formal memorials. Fifty-six years after our riots it is right and just to pause and remember the five days that changed not only a city, but the souls of its residents forever. Every person that I discuss the riots with talks about how they saw the tanks rolling down their street. No matter what part of the city they were in at the time, they saw tanks. Perhaps that image symbolizes for them the moment when they said to themselves, "Yes, this is really bad."

Stories in this collection come from the people who lived through those days, people who still remember and were willing to share their experiences: Annmarie Thomas's story is a vivid recounting of how going to see Stevie Wonder perform became a harrowing rescue mission; the Kimble Family, a mother and two daughters, offer multiple viewpoints of one riotous day; after Sylvia McClain's experience as a teenager looking into the barrel of a National Guardsman's rifle, she later became a civil rights warrior and even joined the Black Panther Party; Elder Minor Palm, Jr., in his 80s, remembers through the prism of both the 1967 and 1943 riots. As a lifelong Detroiter, I am still amazed at how some parts of the city never recovered after the riot. More importantly, some people never recovered. In my conversations with residents who remained in the city in the years following, they all give the same sad shake of the head and shrug of the shoulders. Many are hurt because so many great businesses were lost, but I also pick up a sense of regret, particularly among African Americans, that they somehow missed the opportunity to fill the entrepreneurial void left gaping open after the "white flight." In a sense, I believe, we entered into an Age of Darkness that moved in like a black cloud to hover over our city for decades to come.

In the Summer of 2023, as we see a multitude of redevelopment projects in Detroit taking flight, we can believe that one corner of that dark cloud is lifting. Hopefully, one day it will completely be lifted so that sunlight can once again shine on us all.

—Heather Buchanan, Editor

INTRODUCTION

A while back, the Detroit Writer's Guild was housed on West McNichols in Detroit. It was there that Heather Buchanan and I touched on the subject of writing riot stories in her genealogy writing class. I told her my two sisters had actually been in the '67 riot at the very beginning. Every time I thought of them running amuck amongst the chaos, a comical image came to mind. The serious thought to write something humorous—not grim—called "I Know Who Started the '67 Riot!" occurred years before I'd ever mentioned it to Heather, but needless to say, I just never got around to actually writing it. Heather, on the other hand, had started a publishing company and I knew that when the time would come, she would not only compel people to write their personal riot stories, she would also publish them. Since the time has come, I was also compelled to write my fictitious comical riot tale—only there wasn't anything funny about the only three paragraphs I'd written:

> I couldn't sleep. Winnie, whom I shared a bedroom with, had finally made it home. She and Lisa had partied way past curfew. I was about to wake our parents so they could get whupped, but Lisa wasn't with her. Winnie grabbed my arm as I tried to open our bedroom door. "No!" she said. "You can't say nothin' not 'til you hear what I got to say!" So I stood there in my pajamas and listened intently.
>
> "I threw a Molotov cocktail through the Big Foe's window. I didn't know if them white cops were in that car or not, but I knew I had to get away from there. I couldn't find Sis, so I ran a few blocks 'til I saw the Clairmount bus comin' down the street. I kept looking for Lisa, but I

> was so scared. I hopped the bus and prayed all the way home that Lisa had gotten away."
>
> Winnie trembled the whole time she talked.
>
> It happened after my two sisters had been to their weekly meeting which usually ended up as a party of some sort. They were out having a good time with the brothas and sistahs up on 12th Street. This particular celebration had turned into a stone-cold homecoming for our male relatives and friends who'd just returned from 'Nam, but things had turned sour when the police raided the joint. Winnie made my 12-year -old mind understand why the dudes kept saying: "I'mah so sick and tired of the Big Foe startin' mess!" The 'Nam brothers had their own war to fight at home and were mad about having had to fight someone else's war. She also said that since the Big Foe always raided the meetings, folk in there celebrating were "ready for 'em this time."

Needless to say, my account took on a serious tone. And since there has never been anything comical about Detroit's historical relationship of its predominately white law enforcement and its black community—beginning as early as 1833 with a Wayne County sheriff and two escaped slaves—I decided to keep the tone serious.

During the 1967 riot, the Algiers Motel Incident took place where three young black men were shot to death by members of the Detroit Police Department without probable cause at the motel on Woodward Avenue. The police destroyed two black culture establishments on the westside of Detroit located on Dexter Avenue roughly within the same distance. One business, the Easel Gallery, ran by Glanton Dowdell, the gifted artist who painted the famous Black Madonna portrait, was a small art gallery that contained the works of black artists. According to *Detroit: I Do Mind Dying—A Study in Urban Revolution* updated edition by Dan Georgakas and Marvin Surkin, "during the Great Rebellion, the police destroyed his art gallery, and he was shot at several times." (This writer is not sure if the Easel was a rebuilt gallery. A *Michigan Chronicle* article dated September 9, 1967 written by Betty De Ramus entitled, "Glanton Dowdell: Artist, Drop-Out, Ex-Con, Leader" does not mention any such destruction.) The police also firebombed Vaughn's Bookstore, the only black owned bookstore in the city at that time.

In a phone interview with me in February 2006, former bookstore owner Edward Vaughn said that in 1967 a Sergeant Slaughter of the Detroit Police Department accused him of starting the riot. Vaughn's Bookstore was also accused of being "the headquarters for a black nationalist group" which had been accused "of advocating the violent overthrow of the government." The police also said guns were stored in the bookstore. In the 1999 book entitled *Dancing in the Street: Motown and the Cultural Politics of Detroit*, author Suzanne E. Smith says the police "did not deny their involvement, and instead defended their actions as necessary." She also said a tenth precinct sergeant "admitted firebombing" the bookstore and "justified it as a response to reports that guns were being stored inside."

Vaughn's co-owner, Polly Ross, said that since the bookstore opened, they had been "subjected to a subtle form of harassment by police." Ross also said plainclothes detectives came in often, never purchasing anything for more than 25 cents.

The police actually referred to Forum 66, the Voice of Black Unity, a weekly panel discussion on religion, education, Negro history, literature, drama, music, and the arts, hosted by Vaughn at the bookstore. The forum raised the consciousness of the black community as it prepared for the Detroit Black Arts Conference.

An extensive Chronicle article dated July 29, 1967 titled "Book Store Destroyed, Witnesses Blame Police" written by Aretha Watkins, stated eyewitnesses said the vandals were members of the police department. The police came in three cars around 4:00 a.m. on July 27, 1967. They trained their police lights on the buildings across from the bookstore to see if anyone was watching. When they thought the area was clear, they used rifle butts to break out the bookstore's windows. They went in and wreaked havoc throughout.

In the interview Vaughn said this was the second firebombing. After the police found they had not totally destroyed the bookstore the first time they firebombed it, Vaughn said Slaughter stated they would be back. Books salvaged from the first firebombing—that had been placed back on the shelves—were once again thrown on the floor. Vaughn continued, "This time after the police knocked the books back onto the floor, they went into the bathroom and turned on the water faucets, flooding the bookstore, damaging the total bookstore." Damage to the store was between $5,000-$10,000.

After the second firebombing, the community helped get the bookstore cleaned up, back in order, and stocked again. Vaughn said an article written in Publisher's Weekly generated free books from all over the country to aid the bookstore in its endeavor to rebuild. Vaughn also said that at the time of the Detroit '67 riot, he wasn't even here but at the Black Power Convention held in Newark—and was arrested there for starting the riot back here in Detroit.

Although this book contains personal accounts of both the 1943 and 1967 riots, I felt compelled to show readers a brief spattering of other riots that have occurred in Detroit's history. Two known riots happened in the Nineteenth Century in 1833 and 1863. And in the Twentieth Century, two not so well-known riots happened in 1966 and 1975.

My research found that these four riots were basically motivated by racial tension, fear of change, or lack of acceptance in the status quo. Depending on the research source, a riot may have been termed "insurrection," "incident," "rebellion," or "civil disturbance." But "riot," as defined by Webster's Dictionary, is "a violent public disturbance of the peace, by a number of persons (specified, in law, usually as three or more) assembled together."

1833

The Northwest Territory was defined in the ordinance of 1787 as free, but Negro slavery still existed in Michigan. To name a few slaveholders, GeorgeMcDougall, Joseph Campau, and General John R. Williams (think well known Detroit streets), were leading citizens of Detroit. Because the Michigan Constitution of 1835 prohibited slavery, Detroit was a safe haven for runaway slaves until they could cross the Detroit River to official freedom in Canada.

But if runaways from the South had stayed in Detroit earlier than that—they were not safe because of the Fugitive Slave Law as in the case of Ruth and Thornton Blackburn, two such escaped slaves from Louisville, Kentucky.

According to Clarence M. Burton in his book, *The City of Detroit Michigan 1701-1922 Volume 1* printed in 1922, the majority of Michigan's citizens were law abiding but thought the slave law was "wrong in principle…wantonly cruel, irritating, mischievous and unjust in the methods of its enforcement"— therefore they did not obey it. If a person knew of fugitive slaves in the area he simply did not tell the authorities because "as God was his judge no power on earth could make him assist to enforce a law which he considered morally wrong and an outrage upon the rights of man." However, it was because of attempts to enforce the Fugitive Slave Law that the "Negro Insurrection" occurred on June 16, 1833.

The Blackburns arrived in Detroit in July 1831 and lived as productive citizens for two years before their master discovered their whereabouts. Once in Detroit his slave catcher, sent from Kentucky, contacted Wayne County Sheriff John M. Wilson, who promptly arrested the Blackburns as "fugitives from labor" in order to detain them in a holding cell for the slave catcher's convenience. They were set to leave the same day on the Ohio, a steamer, located on the Detroit River boat dock at the foot of Randolph Street. But some coloureds and whites (there weren't that many, about 400 coloreds to 5,000 whites) were not pleased with any of this and took extreme measures of their own to help the slave couple escape. In the meantime Ruth was able to escape from the jail by switching clothes with Mrs. French, one of two female visitors who came to the jail. She made it all the way to Canada unscathed.

However, freedom for Thornton, who remained in jail until the next day, was not easy to obtain.

According to Reginald Larrie in Corners of Black History, on the next day "shortly before four o'clock in the afternoon, a carriage was driven up to the jail to take Blackburn to the boat." But the delivery was unsuccessful. A melee of folks carried clubs, rocks, and pistols and was able to free Thornton from the law. However, during the melee, the sheriff was badly beaten. He suffered facial cuts, knocked out teeth, and a fractured skull. But whites started a rumor: "The niggers have risen and killed the sheriff!" Whites then attacked any colored person on the street. They also burned forty dwellings to the ground—with the colored occupants still in them. Troops from Fort Gratiot were ordered for crowd control. And as a result of this riot, a group originally created as a "fire watch group" and to keep watch of Indian attacks went on to officially become the Detroit Metropolitan Police Department according to the History of Detroit and Wayne County and Early Michigan written in 1890 by Silas Farmer.

The colored citizens successfully carried out their plan to send the couple to Canada. When Thornton first arrived, however, he was detained in jail for a few days until Canadian officials released him. He eventually joined Ruth and they moved to Toronto, Ontario and became prominent with "considerable property" until their deaths.

1863

In an 1863 editorial in The Christian Recorder, the communication vehicle of the African Methodist Episcopal Church, it was written: "We have to chronicle one of the most disgraceful, inhuman, and heathen-like riots, ever recorded upon the pages of history. It occurred in the city of Detroit,

Michigan....What have the coloured people done that they should be thus treated?"

In truth, the only two things coloured people had done was collectively celebrate the announcement of the Emancipation Proclamation, and individually, one coloured man went to trial for a crime he did not commit. suffered facial cuts, knocked out teeth, and a fractured skull. But whites started a rumor: "The niggers have risen and killed the sheriff!" Whites then attacked any colored person on the street.

They also burned forty dwellings to the ground—with the colored occupants still in them.

Troops from Fort Gratiot were ordered for crowd control. And as a result of this riot, a group originally created as a "fire watch group" and to keep watch of Indian attacks went on to officially become the Detroit Metropolitan Police Department according to the History of Detroit and Wayne County and Early Michigan written in 1890 by Silas Farmer.

The colored citizens successfully carried out their plan to send the couple to Canada. When Thornton first arrived, however, he was detained in jail for a few days until Canadian officials released him. He eventually joined Ruth and they moved to Toronto, Ontario and became prominent with "considerable property" until their deaths.

So, "What made white people start a riot against the coloureds?" should have been the question.

Wilbur Storey, the 1863 editor of The Detroit Free Press, gave whites the ammunition needed to wreak havoc on the coloured community by publishing racist sentiments. He said, according to Dancing in the Street, that "the Civil War was fought not to preserve the Union but to ensure 'nigger domination.'"

However, Matthew Kundinger's twenty-nine page website thesis entitled "Racial Rhetoric: The Detroit Free Press and Its Part in the Detroit Race Riot of 1863" almost defends Storey. "It cannot be determined by the research done thus far whether the Free Press caused the prejudices and violence of its readers; or whether the racism of its readers caused the paper to print what it did," Kundinger stated. Labor, the Civil War, citizenship and morality were the "hot issues" of the day the Free Press used to show how, if coloureds gained by way of them, that made them a threat to Free Press readers who were, at the time, mostly lower class working white males who had little power.

If the coloureds were to gain it would put the whites more at risk. It was mainly Storey's articles about interracial sex that were against the coloureds in the months leading up to the riot. The articles were deliberately written to make the coloureds inferior. According to Kundinger, on February 13, 19, 20 and 21, 1863 articles on amalgamation affairs or "dens" appeared in the *Free Press*. Although whites participated in these events it was because coloureds did too that the articles were extremely derogatory. A week later, on February 27, the Free Press reported the Faulkner case and set the tone even further.

Kundinger stated, "The sub-headline reads, 'A negro entraps a little girl into his room and commits a fiendish crime upon her person.'"

At the end of the Civil War, Detroit's population was 45,000, including approximately 1,400 coloureds. The trial for a man whites weren't even sure was coloured turned out to be the catalyst that set the 1863 race riot off. William Faulkner, the owner of a tavern and eatery, could have been white (because he voted the Democratic ticket when that party was against coloureds), or of Spanish-Indian heritage as he himself claimed to be, or a mulatto. Nonetheless, the *Free Press* repeatedly called him a Negro. Mary Brown, a white girl under the age of eleven, said he raped her and possibly molested Ellen Hoover, her acquaintance of the same age, who was a coloured girl. They had stopped by his establishment to warm their feet while on the way to the post office. (Burton stated, "Faulkner maintained his innocence and his claim came to be generally accepted, as the girl also confessed that it was a 'put up' job. But seven years passed before Faulkner was set free.")

It was the fact that Mary was white and Faulkner, they thought, was coloured that angered whites. It hadn't been enough that Faulkner had been accused, arrested, sent to jail, and faced trial—the whites wanted his blood.

On the first day of his trial, as he was being transported from the jail to the courthouse at Beaubien and Lafayette streets, the white mob tried to snatch him away from the guards to lynch him.

The guards moved him back to the courthouse before dawn to avoid the angry mob again. On this day Faulkner was sentenced to life at Jackson State Prison. Outside a large crowd of "respectable citizens" had gathered outside of the courthouse. They harassed Faulkner and the guards all the way to the jail. Faulkner was hit in the head with a "large paving stone." And since they weren't able to do so, their rally cry of "Kill all the damned niggers!" aided them in ransacking, burning and destroying coloured homes and businesses.

They attacked innocent bystanders as well. Throughout the early part of the day any coloured person—man, woman, or child—"who happened along were subject to kicks, cuffs and blows, and were liable to be butchered upon the streets" by the white mob outside that was much larger than the day before, as they awaited Faulkner's verdict. Detroit's first race riot left two people dead, a multitude of coloureds "savagely attacked," a number of buildings owned by coloureds vandalized and damaged by fires of which thirty-five were burned to the ground.

Troops from Detroit's Fort Wayne and Ypsilanti were called in to quell the riot. According to Dancing, "when the Detroit City Council realized that such drastic measures were needed to restore and maintain peace, it resolved to organize a police department…." As a result, the Detroit Police Department was founded "with one central objective in mind: to contain racial unrest in the city."

1966

The Kercheval Incident was a "mini-riot" that started August 9, 1966. It is not well known but involved conflict with the police who claimed Negro student activists were loitering and causing traffic congestion on Detroit's eastside on Kercheval Street. A Chronicle article, "Question 'Closed' Meetings," dated August 27, 1966, gave a partial statement from an open letter from the Socialist Workers Party to Mayor Jerome P. Cavanagh in defense of the Afro-American Unity Movement and what happened during the Kercheval Incident. "For four days and nights your police flooded a predominantly Negro neighborhood on the Eastside with Tactical Mobile Units, squad car patrols and lines of marching police equipped with shotguns and rifles and fixed bayonets. More than 100 people were arrested. It was like an army occupying 'enemy' territory—virtual martial law. Yet your police commissioner Girardin repeatedly stated that there never was a 'plot' and he even said, 'The elements weren't there for a riot.' But your police harassed a whole neighborhood, created a false picture of terrible danger and then engaged in wholesale arrests and charges of inciting to riot."

At this time, the headquarters of the Afro-American Unity Movement coordinated by Alvin Harrison, was located at 9211 Kercheval and had been under continuous police surveillance because Negroes frequently congregated there "to do something progressive" for their community. Harrison and Dowdell were two men arrested and charged with inciting the riot. Harrison was also charged with conspiracy. Dowdell was also charged with carrying a concealed weapon of which he received a suspended sentence. Dowdell was convicted and placed on five years probation.

After the riot occurred, Citizens Concerned About Police

Harassment on the Eastside was tentatively created to make Negroes in the immediate area and throughout the city aware of the Kercheval Incident. Joseph Barron, Wayne County chairman of the Freedom Now Party, was named the group's temporary chairman of its education committee. From the Chronicle article titled "Group to 'Inform City' Of 'Kercheval Facts,'" dated September 3, 1966, he stated, "We want to make the black community more aware of the attitude of the police and the poor relationships between the black community and the police force, because of the anti-Negro feeling of the police force.

We want to tell them what they can do to change the atmosphere so that this type of incident won't be repeated."

At the time of the Kercheval riot, just around the corner on Harding Street, Coleman Young (at the time of his senate campaign) held a wake for his father at his father's house. A police officer friend of his called and informed him of the incident going down in the area and suggested that he move his friends and family away from the area for their safety. Disgruntled about the police situation on Kercheval and its disruption of his father's wake, Young used his clout and called on his political brother, U.S. Congressman Charles Diggs, some other elected officials, ministers, and community leaders of whom were mostly Negro, and a few whites. Soon, there were about sixty of them "marching arm in arm down Kercheval" as a means to protest law enforcement's presence. In *Hard Stuff: The Autobiography of Coleman Young*, co-authored with Lonnie Wheeler in 1994, Young stated, "As we walked, a cavalcade of tactical mobile units—police cruisers—pulled up alongside, rumbling along very slowly, bumper to bumper" as they kept their eyes on the group. One of the officers snarled at them and said, "You goddamn niggers get your black asses off the street."

It is important to note that the Michigan Civil Rights Commission documented 32 cases of police brutality against Negroes since 1964. The July 2, 1966 Chronicle article, "CRC Report Cites Police Bias," stated numerous types of complaints namely, "harassment tactics, such as, stopping and questioning citizens on the street; searching and arresting citizens without cause and without suspicion of wrongdoing; verbal abuse, such as derogatory racial remarks, use of profane language, lack of courtesy, insulting comments and inappropriate use of first names; and physical abuse, from shoving and pushing to beating."

Of even greater note, three weeks after the civil rights report article, and roughly two weeks before the Kercheval Incident, "Can It Happen in Detroit?" a Chronicle article dated July 23, 1966 appeared. It posed the question to local leaders and "ghetto dwellers." The dwellers believed police brutality and youth restlessness could cause a mass riot because in other cities it only took one minor incident to set a riot off. Even Mayor Cavanagh had this to say: "Detroiters would only be kidding themselves if they said it can't happen here. It always can happen when frustration mounts along with the thermometer."

Besides the Kercheval Incident, a few other incidents occurred in Detroit in 1966 that were reported. All involved the police and Negro citizens. The July 23 article continued: "Several skirmishes broke out on Belle Isle recently when reportedly unruly citizens were forced to disperse by police, adding fuel to riot fears. Over the week-end, witnesses charged that an injured man, who mistakenly assaulted a plainclothes officer on Third and Temple, had been viciously beaten before an interracial group of about 100 persons. One witness admitted that had the beating continued he was 'ready to die.'"

1975

The Livernois Fenkell Incident, considered a "minor riot," started around 8:30 p.m. on July 28, 1975 and lasted two days. It had been claimed by 39-year-old Andrew Chinarian, the white owner of Bob Bolton's Bar & Grill, 14907 Livernois at Chalfonte near Fenkell, that three black teenagers tried to steal a car in the bar's parking lot. He fired one shot and a bullet hit 18-year-old Obie Wynn, whom Chinarian claimed held an "object," in the back of the head. Blacks inside the bar, who witnessed the shooting, looted the bar. They also set the carpet on fire. Directly after Wynn had been taken to Mt. Carmel

Mercy Hospital, things got out of hand quickly as word spread throughout the community. However, as witnesses to the 1967

Detroit riot, older blacks were not up to any devastation. Once they knew Chinarian was in custody they relaxed a little. It was the young blacks who started the looting, burning, and rock throwing after a report came out around 10:00 p.m. that Chinarian had been released without being charged. "For the next several hours rocks were thrown and windows were broken along a mile stretch of Livernois. Six looting incidents were also reported," stated the August 2, 1975 Chronicle article, "Cops Hailed For Averting Riot," written by Brian Flanigan. A police officer, fireman, and Chronicle columnist Jim Ingram were also injured from thrown rocks. Police cars were vandalized, set on fire, or overturned. At least one civilian car was also overturned. A police helicopter was hit by shotgun pellets.

The crowd, police said, gathered 300 people.

When Coleman A. Young, then the newly appointed first black mayor of the city of Detroit, heard of the incident, he decided right then and there to stop the madness. He knew that if the predominately white police force of the past "had gone about cracking heads in the Detroit tradition, there would have been hell to pay." Young commanded then Police Chief Philip Tannian to call in all black police officers and merge them with the white officers already on the scene to give the department an air of racial unification. The mayor also stated in Hard Stuff, "That may have been the first time in Detroit history that black officers had been called upon for emergency police work."

But no matter the color of the officer, blacks, in an era of "off the pigs," continued to disrespect the uniform. They threw bottles and rocks at the police officers who had been commanded not to fire their guns. Racial fighting occurred on both Livernois and Fenkell streets, at the time a racially mixed area. The mayor put himself on the line by fighting "attitude with attitude."

He spoke angrily at the black crowd as he stood on top of a parked car. He called some of them a bunch of "hoodlums and rip-off artists." The mayor was heckled by the crowd. Someone hit him with a rock, but eventually things calmed down. He also caught it from three white police officers who rode up in a cruiser and threw a smoke bomb underneath a car next to where he and some other police personnel stood. Young and the officers with him jumped into a "sympathetic" inspector's car and chased after them, but couldn't catch up with them.

Somewhere along the line however, the crowd of angry blacks regressed. Although Mayor Young walked the streets in the area and talked constantly to black youth to convince them not to burn the stores in the area, they still wanted to burn down Chinarian's bar. And they wanted the bar owner's blood.

They rammed his bar with the intent to drag him out to do bodily harm but they were unsuccessful. Instead, around 11:30 p.m., three Detroit men pulled and dragged 54-year-old Marian Pyszko, an innocent white male of Polish descent, from his car as he drove in the area from work to home—and used a large chuck of concrete to stone him; he died three days later. "Mini-Riot Victim's Rites," another *Chronicle* article written by Flanigan dated August 9, 1975, stated Ronald Bell Jordan, Raymond Peoples, and Dennis Lindsay were all later charged with first degree murder in Pyszko's death.

The next day, after it was reported that Wynn had died, and that "Chinarian had been rearrested and charged with second degree murder by Recorder's Court Presiding Judge Donald Leonard who imposed a bond of $500 and two sureties," the angry black crowd threw rocks, burned and looted again.

However, once Leonard obtained the coroner's report that Wynn had, indeed, been shot in the back of the head, he called a second hearing and reset Chinarian's bond at $25,000 of which Chinarian paid and was released again.

Even with respected community leaders keeping the crowd abreast of changes, they still wanted to retaliate because, in their eyes, justice had not been served.

Because Young had joined the merged police force along with clergymen and other community leaders, the riot that "threatened to escalate into a fullscale disturbance" was quelled before it became full-blown. Damage to the area was estimated at "tens of thousands of dollars," yet as recent as this riot was, few Detroiters know about it.

—Teresa "Teki" Kimble

“Hurry, come on, Detroit is on fire!”

ANNMARIE THOMAS

I was only thirteen years old on the day the riot erupted in Detroit, Michigan. My oldest sister, two cousins, a friend of mine and myself were attending the Motown Revue at the Fox Theatre. Stevie Wonder was performing on the stage when suddenly we could hear my mother's voice screaming my sister's and my name loudly. We had no idea what was going on; so embarrassed we slid down in our seats to hide because we could hear the laughter from the audience.

As an usher directed my mother and a next door neighbor into the Fox's auditorium, my mother finally spotted us and gestured to us to get up from our seats because, as my mother put it,

“Hurry, come on, Detroit is on fire!”

I remember looking up and seeing the fear in my mother's face as we all immediately left our seats and followed behind my oldest cousin and my sister as to protect the end of the group from the unknown emergency we were about to face. When we exited the theater building I could see gray thick smoke that streaked the blue summer sky. Sirens could be heard in all directions. We were terrified, but Mrs. Maclin, our next door neighbor, started up her car and took off through all the commotion, trying to get us all home safely.

As we entered Woodward Avenue, we were directed to many different detours because buildings were burning, and people were wildly running in the streets seemingly to escape the disaster that we observed from the moving car. There were many police officers, certainly more than I had ever witnessed in my young teen years.

I could feel the fear inside of me, and as I looked into my cousins', sister's and friend's eyes I knew that they were experiencing some fear also. We finally made it to West Grand Boulevard. While passing

12th Street, I could see the fierce black smoke that covered the sky, indicating danger to anyone making a right turn off of West Grand to 12th.

My mother kept telling us, "We're going to be alright, we're almost home."

As we approached West Grand Boulevard and Linwood we watched people running in the streets with television sets and food from the A&P grocery store. The large window of the store was smashed as we watched people climb into the opening made by bricks and other objects that would break a large sized window. We continued to hear the sirens of fire trucks and police cars.

Finally reaching Lawton, Mrs. Maclin made a right turn to get us to our destination, Northwestern Street. I remember seeing familiar faces running toward West Grand maybe to loot or observe the insanity of an out of control situation.

When we got closer to Northwestern we could see that Chris's Party Store on Lawton and Northwestern had also been invaded by looters helping themselves to merchandise that was purchased by a family who owned the business and had always been kind to neighbors who supported the business.

We finally arrived home safely, stunned from what we had just witnessed. My mother frantically made phone calls to my father and oldest brother to make sure they were okay at their jobs. She then explained to us that she had heard that the Detroit S.T.R.E.S.S. Unit had beaten an African American man to death so there was an outrage from other African Americans who were tired of the unjust treatment they had been receiving from the special unit of the police department.

The beginning of a peaceful Saturday turned out to be a disaster as five frightened girls went upstairs and got on our knees and began to pray. We looked from our bedroom window to see smoke of fires from blocks away rapidly digesting the sky with fumes of heavy smoke. We were so afraid that our neighborhood would be destroyed as well.

The National Guard was ordered to survey the city for law and order, but the killing and looting did not stop the first two days of the riot, as I recall. I remember it was reported that suspected snipers had been shooting at police officers and National Guardsmen from the roof of a building on Linwood and Hogarth. A man was shot and killed by officers along with other individuals on 12th Street where the disturbance was supposed to have originated.Stores and homes were destroyed from the devastating riot of 1967

My girlfriend's cousin's home on Calvert off of 12th was burned to the ground and their family had to temporarily move in with my girlfriend and her family. The number of deaths and injuries mounted as the city continued to be controlled by the National Guard. Innocent people lost their lives during this disruption, even innocent children.

As we sat on our porch while a curfew was enforced, I remember waving to the men who drove down Northwestern in army jeeps followed by army tanks. In the early part of the day we were allowed to take short walks up to Northwestern High School's field. The green army vehicles canvassed the entire field.

The neighborhoods were like a ghost town of ruined buildings with no employees working on a usual workday. Grand River no longer displayed Red Robin clothing store, Cunningham's and other businesses that were completely destroyed. There was very little merchandise left to pick up from the ruins, but our father forbade us to bring any merchandise in our home that was not paid for.

My cousin visiting from Ducan, Pennsylvania, called her parents every day, reporting the news of what she surprisingly was experiencing on her vacation in Detroit. Chris's family, owners of the corner party store on Lawton and Northwestern, never came back to the neighborhood to pass out free candy when the children who lived there received an "A" or "B" on their report cards. Even the handful of candy that was given away on Halloween night was obsolete for the children after the riot.

Yes, Detroit was in turmoil in the summer of '67'. This was a part of history that I will always remember, and as I relive the scenes of the 1967 Detroit Riot while writing this essay, I think about the flourishing buildings that once served and occupied a once family-oriented community.

Now, when I visit my mother's home I only have memories of the stores, shoe repair shops, and apartment buildings on Linwood and Northwestern. For the last thirtysomething years, the buildings have been replaced with lifeless vacant lots that may never see the reconstruction of a neighborhood that once told the story of a historical moment in Detroit, 1967.

“Are we going to die?
We’re the good kids, not the bad ones.
Lord, please keep us safe to go home.”

SYLVIA McCLAIN

Riot 101: 1967

My friends and I were running south on 12th Street in July 1967. Just one block more to go and then we heard it.

“Stop right where you are,” said the armed white man. We didn’t stop. We froze in our tracks. And that is when the fear took over as the lights flashed before the eyes of this fourteen-year-old black female child.

The first thing that came to my mind was, *Are we going to die? Can’t they see we are trying to get home right now? We’re the good kids, not the bad ones. Lord, please keep us safe to go home.* It didn’t matter, though. Two armored tanks came to a stop and they jumped out. National Guardsmen jumped out with M60s in their hands pointed straight at us, four kids just trying to get around the corner to home. The armed National Guardsmen were white and we were black.

We were at the cross streets of Cortland and 12th, just around the corner from our homes on Richton. We never knew that a couple of minutes past our curfew would put our lives in so much danger.

The riot had started a few days earlier one mile south of Richton Street at 12th and Clairmount. The market on the corner of our street had already been burned down. Two dry cleaners had already had break-ins and clothing stolen. After dark, you could hear the firearms go off as you heard the yelling and screaming of the armed men and citizens. The Riot of 1967 was never going to be forgotten by me, let alone my friends.

There were four of us: two females and two males. One guard walked over to one of the males and asked him what he was doing out after curfew. He attempted to turn and face the guard to explain and was shoved against the brick building with all four M60s appearing suddenly right in his face. I recall hearing a guard shouting something like, "Did we say you could turn around?" My friend responded with a no and then pressed his face onto the brick walled building. That's when a guard came over to me and shouted in my face. I don't recall what it was he said, because at that point I was so scared, I wet my jeans. Yet, the muzzle of a firearm pressed against the temple of my head was confirmation enough of the danger we were in. We were part of a riot going on in Detroit.

The guards started laughing and told us to turn around and face them. The four of us did as we were told. We were then instructed to look them in the face. They asked us where we lived. In unison, we said on the next street as we all pointed south to the corner. One guard asked us why we were not home already. One friend replied we had lost track of time at the playground on Woodrow Wilson and that was why we were running home.

After a couple of minutes of discussion between themselves, the guards decided to let us go. They told us to start running and that we had all of one minute to get around the corner or we would be sorry. Understanding the words between the lines spoken, we took off like airplanes down a runway at the airport. I don't even remember getting to my house. I only remember sitting on the porch that night watching the tanks going north on 12th Street. I remember seeing the news the next day on television and the pictures of beaten bodies on the streets of Detroit. I remember thinking that could have been my friends and me. We could have become part of the six-o'clock news.

The Riot of 1967 in Detroit was a learning lesson for me. Racial attitudes still existed between blacks and whites. Mistrust by blacks of whites with guns was a harbored emotion. We were teenagers of the Sixties living the discrimination stories of the south told by blacks raised during the Fifties. All I knew was that the stories became a reality for me in the north. I, along with other teenagers, had then thought blatant harassment was a thing of the past. Yet, four teenagers personally experienced harassment during the '67 riot. We no longer would be a new generation of blacks with hope for the future.

After that incident, I became very active in civil rights issues. I joined the Black Panther Party. I protested at every function that involved the rights of blacks. I purposely took part in establishing student and neighborhood organizations. From that point on, I never saw things with rose-colored glasses anymore. I was an unwitting victim of the riot in Detroit in 1967 and would never be the same fourteen-year-old girl again. I grew up and became what I am today, a black woman that accepts no harassment, discrimination, prejudice, nor blatant racial discord. As the singer Helen Reddy said in her '70s song, "I am woman hear me roar!"

Now, nearly four decades later, Affirmative Action has been struck down here in Michigan. Each battle won in the fight for equality is to be erased from the collective minds of past warriors. We now know that the feelings felt by some whites in the Sixties never were resolved. The war against inequality is still going on.

I truly hope that there will be no unrest like that of the Sixties. Another riot is the worst that could happen, but only time will tell.

Sharon Stanford

12th Street & *The Grapes of Wrath*

The summer of 1967 was one of the best summers of my life. It was the year that I turned sixteen. In my fevered teenage mind, the parties, the picnics, having my first job and an extended summer vacation because of one of Detroit's perpetual teacher strikes made it a season to remember. Even having to go to summer school so that I could take fewer classes my senior year did not interfere with my fun. I was blissfully unaware of the pervasive racism and resentment that was simmering in my city.

We lived in a middle class eastside neighborhood. There were Germans, Poles, Jews and other ethnic groups in our neighborhood and in the schools my sisters and I attended. Most, if not all, of the stores and businesses in our area were owned by white people. In fact, the only aberration was a small grocery store around the corner from our house that we referred to as "the colored store," because it was owned by a Negro. We didn't shop there very often, but it had the best penny candy.

I distinctly remember that hot July Sunday when the riot broke out. I was returning from the Eastown Theatre on Harper and Van Dyke with my friends, Linda and Antoinette. We had gone there to see the latest Beach Party or Elvis movie. I don't remember which. The most important part of going to the movies on Sunday afternoon was to see who was there with who and who was making out with whom.

Dressed in our Sunday best, minus hats and gloves, we were walking down Van Dyke and we could smell smoke, lots of smoke. There was an unnatural feeling in the air. Then we noticed people, mostly young men, leaving out of the stores on Van Dyke (which were closed on Sundays in those days), the Cunningham's drugstore and the record store, carrying handfuls of merchandise. In those days, television sets were too big and heavy to carry. The biggest object you could carry was a transistor radio. We heard people mumbling about a "race riot" and the police shooting Negroes.

Somewhat alarmed, but still unaware of what was going on, we headed down Medbury. I lived off Medbury on Iroquois, and Linda and Antoinette lived on the next street, Seneca. As I turned onto Iroquois, I could see my grandfather standing out in the middle of the sidewalk, looking anxiously up and down the street. Upon seeing me, he motioned for me to hurry up and get in the house and told Linda and Antoinette to go straight home. Still confused, I went up on the porch of our house. My grandmother was sitting on the porch, looking anxious also.

"It's another riot," she murmured. "I don't believe this is happening again."

Of course I didn't know that she was referring to 1943. It was only after watching the television and reading the newspaper that I found out there had been a "race riot" in Detroit in 1943.

The next few days were unreal. We learned that police had raided a blind pig, an illegal after-hours club, on 12th Street. Someone started shooting and bricks were thrown at police cars and suddenly, Detroit was on the national news. Buildings were burning and people were looting. On television, we saw tanks rolling down the streets of Detroit. The National Guard had been sent to our city.

We were not allowed to leave our street. At the most, we could sit on the porch and chat with our neighbors. At night we didn't turn on any lights in the house for fear of (as my grandfather said) someone "chucking a rock through the window." We played checkers and Movie Stars (a game my sister made up) or read in the semi-darkness of the streetlights on Iroquois.

One evening, bored with the tedium, I turned on the TV. For whatever reason, everyone had gone to bed, except me. The movie, *The Grapes of Wrath*, was on. I became enthralled in the story of the Joad Family and their struggle during the Depression. What impressed me the most was that I didn't know that white people could be poor and struggling. I had seen a few struggling Negro families (not realizing that our family was one.) I didn't know that white people could be so poor and broken down. I also wondered briefly why these folks didn't get on "the welfare," as my grandmother called it. I didn't know what "the welfare" was at the time, but I knew that the lady down the street with all the kids was on it. Sometimes she even came down and borrowed five or ten dollars from my grandmother while she waited for her next check.

Abruptly, my grandfather came downstairs in his pajamas and ordered me to turn off the TV. "Somebody'll chuck a rock in the window if they see a light on," he admonished me. I could have protested, but being an obedient child I did as I was told. It really bothered me that I didn't find out if the Joads found jobs or got on the welfare.

"There was an unnatural feeling in the air..."

After the riot, life changed. The grocer on the corner, the drugstore, the cleaners, all closed. I never saw white people clear out of a city so fast. Slowly, but surely, the white people on our street began to move to something called "the suburbs."

Our practically all-white police department in the city began to change also. More Negroes were recruited to the force. No more would an all-white force be allowed to persecute the Negro citizens of the city. Many things changed in the next few years. The next year, Martin Luther King, Jr. and Robert Kennedy were assassinated. President Lyndon B. Johnson introduced his "Great Society" that revealed the ugly underbelly of poverty in America. On television we saw poor white people like the ones in *The Grapes of Wrath*. James Brown implored Negroes to be black and proud; suddenly, everyone was sprouting huge Afros and dashikis and talking about Mother Africa. Protests against the Vietnam War and apartheid in South Africa were happening everywhere. It was a wonderful, terrible time in America and I took it all in.

By the way, it was years before I finally saw the end of *The Grapes of Wrath*. It didn't end like I thought it would. The Joad Family was still struggling and Tom Joad was on the run from the law. Kind of like life, I guess: sometimes there's a happy ending, but most of the time, we just continue to struggle and survive. But we do, indeed, survive.

WANDA (KIMBLE) KEYS

MERCY, MERCY ME
(Things Ain't What They Used to Be. . .)

The sun was beginning to rise at 5:15 a.m. on Sunday, July 23, 1967. It was going to be a typical hot and humid summer day in Detroit, Michigan. At this hour of the morning, my sister Laverne, my best friend Dana, my cousin Harvey and I were just getting home from a party at one of our cousin's homes. We were teenagers who had stayed out way past the allowable curfew. In retrospect, I can't imagine what kind of partying we were doing that had us still out at this hour of the morning. I was only nineteen.

My sister Laverne drove her 1963 tan Dodge. We were riding east on Clairmount Street. She stopped the car just long enough for Harvey to get out of the car; he lived right on our route home. He stayed with his mother, father and brothers in a large, brick two-family flat that was located right on the corner of Clairmount and 14th Streets. He got out, hurled a few insults at us, and Laverne drove off.

Laverne proceeded east down Clairmount. We noticed the sound of burglar alarms ringing in the distance. Not one burglar alarm, but the sound of many. This was strange, because a burglar alarm ringing back then meant somebody had the nerve to break into something and the police would soon be arriving. This did not happen often.

As we approached the next stoplight, which was 12th Street, the alarms got louder. We glanced down 12th to see people running and shouting. Alarms were ringing like mad—*but, there were no police!* That was extremely odd.

Our teenage curiosity (or absence of good sense), coupled with the fact that we had been drinking beer, got the best of us. Laverne parked the car a safe distance away and we actually got out of the car and walked the block or two where the action was. We stood on the sidewalk across the street from the action and watched in amazement.

Nobody bothered us and we stayed the hell out of the way, but we wanted to see and know what was happening. Even though what we were witnessing was very strange and even dangerous, we felt no real fear for our personal safety because back then people would rarely hurt anyone, especially three teenaged girls, for no reason at all. What we saw were people running in and out of a few stores that had been broken into. The large front plate glass windows, which were next to the entrance to most of the small neighborhood businesses in those days, had been smashed in with bricks. I remember a pawnshop, a furniture store and a drugstore were being hit as we stood and watched. Some of the doors of the stores, which were only protected by alarms in those days, were kicked in or smashed in. People were helping themselves to whatever they could
carry.

Across the street from where we were standing, I saw a man come out of a store with a portable TV hoisted on his shoulder; he proceeded to walk down the street with it. I saw a lady going down another street carrying a living room chair; a boy walking behind her was carrying a chair justlike the one she had. Why not get a set? I wondered. People were coming out of the liquor store with bottles of booze and cigarettes. People were excited, rushing in and out, grabbing all they could. It was like a scene from the old scifi show, "The Twilight Zone." I was waiting to hear Rod Serling's familiar voice-over explaining that what we were seeing was only a scene from the show. But I didn't hear Rod, nor did I hear the crazy theme song from "The Twilight Zone": doo-doo-doo-doo/doo-doo-doo-doo!

At first, we stayed on the sidelines and observed the melee. I kept wondering why the police had not come. And why did everyone seem so fearless? Where did that man get the nerve to carry a TV down a street that he had obviously stolen? A lady walking down the street with a few pieces of furniture for her living room? Come on, now. It was 1967 in Detroit—this sort of stuff did not happen.

We asked someone (I don't remember exactly who) what was going on. We were told that a few hours before, the police raided an after-hours joint (blind pig) a few blocks away. We were told that onlookers and residents who witnessed the raid were angry that the police treated the persons who were arrested with extreme cruelty, beating some of the men and throwing the women into the paddy wagon. People were mad and thus were retaliating. Of course I didn't say anything, but it didn't make sense to me. I couldn't connect what seemed to be two totally different events. What did the raid on the after-hours joint have to do with what was going on in front of my face? I did not have the answer right then.

"Mob mentality" is very real. I found this out as we witnessed the crowd grow larger and more brazen. It was getting crazier and crazier. It was a free-for-all. Well, I got the crazies, too. As I was watching everybody else load up on free goodies, I wanted to see what I could get; after all, the stores were wide open, so it wasn't really stealing.

"'Mob mentality' is very real. . . It was getting crazier and crazier. It was a free-for-all. Well, I got the crazies, too."

Dana, Laverne and I got our nerve up and ran into the corner drugstore. It was full of folks rushing and grabbing merchandise off the shelves. Somebody said, "Ya'll go on in and get some of this free stuff." It was sheer madness! There was broken glass all over the place and I had to be careful not to step on the huge chunks of glass. The burglar alarm was ringing. I was scared as I ran in, but once I was in, I didn't know what the heck to do. I grabbed a handful of jars of Arrid cream deodorant with "Per-Stop" ("Per-Stop" was an ingredient in the deodorant that its advertisers claimed would stop perspiration in its tracks.) My sister grabbed a few fifths of Johnny Walker Red liquor. I don't remember what, if anything, Dana grabbed.

My adrenaline was flowing, but I started to get afraid, too.

Things were out of hand and there was madness in the air. Even as a teenager, I knew we could get into trouble if we got caught up in this mess. We all knew better. Something told all three of us at the same time that we should get the hell out of there. It was fear. We left with our stolen goods and rushed back to the car. Laverne put her foot "to the pedal and the pedal to the metal" and started towards home.

I remember looking back out of the rear window of the car as Laverne drove away from that scene, and I knew I was witnessing something that would be talked about for days. What I saw was a crowd that was growing larger and more aggressive. The absence of fear was the weird thing that set my nerves on edge. Out of the rear window, I saw people carrying food, furniture, clothing—anything they could carry. I saw a man and woman each lugging a couch down the street. Maybe some people went home and came back for more goodies. People were running in and out of the stores and yelling.

As we maneuvered our way back to Clairmount, which was only two blocks away, we found it was eerily quiet outside of that tiny area where we had just left. The ride home was uneventful. It seemed like a typically slow Sunday morning; the rest of the city was just waking up, oblivious to what was happening on 12th Street. No police cars were rushing past us to the scene where we had just left. Nothing. I would liken our ride home to being in an active war zone and then walking a few blocks away and finding peace and quiet. It did indeed seem like a scene from "The Twilight Zone." I was glad to be on our way home.

The ride home took about ten minutes. By the time we made it, we were excited and frightened about the chaos that we had just witnessed. My mother was awake and she was shocked to find out her girls had been out all night long. But as we started telling her what we'd seen—minus our part in it—she told us she had heard about some trouble at an after-hours joint on the radio. She explained why the crowd outside of the place was so angry: black people were tired of being treated so brutally by the police all the time.

She told us she was glad we had sense enough to come on home.

So, it was more to it than just a crowd of angry people. It went much deeper than that. I still couldn't find the correlation. I was tired and went to bed around 6:30 a.m. When I awoke a few hours later, I finally began to understand the connection between the after-hours joint and the chaos on 12th Street.

By that Sunday evening the mayhem on 12th Street had made the news on both TV and radio. The black radio stations were talking about the rioting and looting. They were warning people to stop and go home, and if you were already home to stay there. People were being warned to stay away from the area. Neighbors were talking. When we told our neighborhood friends what we had witnessed and took part in that very morning, they thought we were crazy. Relatives were calling to check on each other. We were told to stay close to home. And we did. The police did not try to break up the mayhem—I heard they thought the situation would wear itself down.

Three days later, sections of Detroit were on fire. Clouds of smoke hung in the air. We went to bed with the smell of smoke. The National Guard was called in. I remember two National Guardsmen, who looked to be no older than me, running through our backyard with their rifles positioned on their shoulders, pointing upwards. They were looking for looters, I imagined. They scared the hell out of my mother and us. And they looked as scared as we were.

At night, my mother used the water hose to wet down the front of our home in case any embers from the burning buildings on Oakland Avenue, just a block away, drifted eastward towards our home. The Big Four became a regular sight in our neighborhood. The Big Four were four policemen who rode around in a black unmarked police car, each with a long rifle hanging out of each of the front car windows. They wanted us to see those rifles. Nobody wanted The Big Four around and nobody messed with them.

The city was almost at a standstill. It was a very dangerous time. People still went to work, if they could. I was afraid for my father. It was good he worked close enough to home that he could walk to work and in the opposite direction of all the trouble. I was afraid for any of my family to leave the house. We were all afraid. Afraid for our young men. Afraid for our property. It was a fearful time.

Detroit made the national news. It took weeks to get the unrest under control. After the smoke cleared, many of the vibrant businesses that were part of our neighborhood were gone, burned to the ground. It was mostly the white-own businesses that were destroyed.

Our neighborhood, as we had known it, was gone in a matter of a few days. Our houses were still standing, but there were gaping holes in the landscape on Oakland Avenue. We needed and used all of those businesses. At the five-and-dime store you could buy everything from a sewing needle to a piece of furniture. If you had a little money, you could choose from a lot of merchandise: a bottle of nail polish, a powder sponge, eyebrow pencils, stockings, hand cream, face powder, fragrance, and Cashmere Bouquet talcum powder. There were sheets, pillowcases, bed linen, bedspreads, dishtowels, pots and pans.

Directly across the street from the five-and-dime was a grocery store. Just about everyone in the neighborhood shopped there almost on a daily basis. Here, some neighbors were even allowed to run a "tab" until payday. Dana's family had a tab. I remember so many days walking into the store with her to purchase something for their dinner on credit. It was not a big deal. That grocery store was looted and burned. Gone was the shoe shop, and next door to that, the dry cleaner. All of these businesses were located on Oakland Avenue, between Hague and Alger, just up the street. Because we lived right across the street from the Moore School playground, which extended from Cameron to the alley at Oakland, we had a very clear picture of the melee. Mason's Funeral Home, on the corner of Oakland and Alger, was spared. Mr. Mason, the owner, was a black man. On the other corner at Oakland and Hague was Barthwell's Drugstore, another black-owned business that was spared.

"It was a fearful time."

Mr. Barthwell* was well known and respected in our community. As children it was such a treat to go into Barthwell's, as it was called. The store had a very special lunch counter where patrons could sit down and order delicious hamburgers, French fries, fresh malts, hand-dipped ice cream, and orange sherbet. I would give anything to be able to visit a store like Barthwell's today.

I look back on that early morning in July of 1967. Things got way out of control over a matter of days. It wasn't a spontaneous event; it was something that was fueled over days. The way I would explain the beginning of the 1967 riot would be that it started off as a small campfire that somebody neglected to put out. Neglected, the campfire grew in a matter of a few days into a huge uncontrollable forest fire.

That's it, Ladies and Gentlemen. I was there. I saw.

*Sidney Barthwell, pharmacist, built the country's largest chain of black-owned-drugstores in Detroit during the 1930's and 1940's. He helped establish the city's African American middle class during that time period.

BRENDA CORNISH

The Detroit "War" of 1967—Who Really Won?

It was in July of 1967 when life, as we knew it in the city of Detroit, changed. It was three years after the tragic car accident that took the life of my father and left me, my mother and siblings healing our wounds and adjusting to our new life without him. My uncle, who had been discharged from Vietnam, came to stay with us that July. My mother felt she could use the help.

My father had purchased our Martindale home in 1957. Our home sat between Grand River and Joy Road, a prosperous area that included clothing stores, shoe stores, drug stores, bakeries and businesses such as real estate, doctor and lawyer offices, all employing from the neighborhood. The Riviera Theater was the landmark for the community as it once had a high-end status much like the Fox Theatre in downtown Detroit today. In 1967, it had become a movie house, still standing grand over the striving businesses surrounding it.

It was on a Sunday afternoon on July 23, 1967, that I asked to go play over my friend Cynthia Hill's house down the street. My mother and Cynthia's mother were best friends so I had no problem being allowed to visit. I remember Cynthia and I playing in their upstairs Sunderoom, when we heard a lot of noise and looked out the window to see what was going on. From this room, we were looking out over Beverly Street where Good Housekeeping sat on the corner of Grand River and Beverly. Being almost ten, we couldn't see much but I remember hearing a man yell, "Here they come!" A few minutes later we heard a lot of glass breaking and could see people running with merchandise. The crowd had hit the Good

Housekeeping store and The Land of Hi-Fi appliance store that sat on the corner of Martindale and Grand River.

Mrs. Hill ran upstairs and got us away from the windows. I remember asking what was going on, but got no answer. Mrs. Hill had Cynthia's big brother, Michael, to walk me home; as we were walking down the street towards the Joy Road end, I kept trying to look behind me at what was going on at the store on the corner. Michael just told me to turn around and keep walking. As the Land of Hi-Fi began to roar into a blaze, I knew a war had begun.

> ". . . we waved at the soldiers and they would cheerfully smile and wave back. . . I believed we all knew they would easily kill us in an instant."

It might have been the third day of the riots when the military presence was everywhere in the city. They rode our streets with their weapons displayed on tanks and jeeps. As children, seeing the strangeness of all this, we waved at the soldiers and they would cheerfully smile and wave back. But, silently, I believed we all knew they would easily kill us in an instant.

About the fourth night of the riot, our family had to take cover as gunfire disturbed our evening. My uncle immediately had us to get down on the floor in fear that our windows would be shot out. The gunfire appeared to be coming from houses around us. It was so intense, my uncle said, he felt like he was back in Vietnam. We crawled on our stomachs from room to room. Finally, when the gunfire slowly subsided, my younger brother and I were allowed to get in one of the beds while the rest of the family slept on the floor.

When we got up the next day and went outside, we found what seemed like hundreds of bullet shells everywhere. My mother's flower garden had been trampled and was littered with bullet shell casings. The neighbor's yards also shared our invasion. As a child, I never knew who or why there was so much gunfire that night. No one we knew had been shot, nor did anyone's home get shot into. But I will always remember seeing the machine guns that were set up behind our house in an open field that has now been covered by a church. My mother said if they had opened up on the homes with those guns, we would have been dead.

Yes, a war had begun. What started out as a protest fueled with anger against racism or (a racist system in the city), became a war – Detroit Negroes against the "System". In getting back at the "System", we battled, pilfered, and burned. Some even died. As a result, some of the resolutions we received were racially sensitive social programs, state scholarships, and diversity in the police department. The war was over—or was it?

Typically, when a war is over, resources come to rebuild the destroyed areas. But Grand River and Joy Road never regained its class or style. The many businesses that employed people from the neighborhood, which allowed residents to walk to work, are now gone. Drugs were now poured into the community, becoming the new neighborhood employer. In fact, Grand River and Joy Road became infamous as the launching area for the organized youth drug ring, Young Boys Incorporated.

The 1967 riot was an explosion of emotional frustration. In hindsight, we can say that things could have been handled better as many black businesses were also lost in the flames that summer—businesses that had survived racist attacks and threats. As a result of our explosion, more dependence on the "system" emerged. We have limited shopping in our neighborhoods, reducing revenues in our city that could have been used for our enhancements. Many neighborhoods still have vacant lots where employing businesses once stood. But our most important demise is that our children do not see prosperity in their neighborhoods, which would have given them the vision to pursue in the same manner.

So, who really won?

RONALD BUCHANAN

The Buffalo and the National Guard

My wife and I were just returning to Detroit from a peaceful three months in Oklahoma in 1967 when we found ourselves in the midst of the riot. I had been in the army for about a year and was scheduled to be shipped off to Vietnam within the next couple of weeks. I first heard about the riot at the airport.

Little did we know that in Oklahoma our days of my coming home to a little house to find her waiting there would be something to treasure. Life was simple there: for the hot Oklahoma days we were issued something just short of an air conditioner, a little gadget that blew water against a fan, turning it into a cool mist. At quiet little picnics, we watched the buffalo roam right before us. In the cool evenings, we joined other young couples outdoors, sitting around campfires where we socialized.

The day we were to return to Detroit, I went to the administration office to pick up my papers. The Administrative Officer, reading my papers, said,

"Detroit? You know they're rioting in Detroit. I wonder why they are burning their own city down."

In defense, I told him what he could do with that comment. Driving to Detroit from Metro Airport, then Inkster (my parents' home), we did not see anything wrong until we got closer to the Davison Freeway. We were headed to my wife's parents' home, just across Davison, on Dearing, a street bordering Hamtramck, a predominately Polish city at the time. On the Davison service drive heading towards the Hamilton exit, we were shocked to see a large crowd of people.

At first, the people were just standing around, and then a large noise, a shot, rang out. Immediately, the crowd started moving all in one direction, then in another direction. My wife and I needed to get across the street, but I sensed that our window of opportunity was small.

Fearfully, my wife asked, "You're going to drive through that?" I remember that she was wearing all white.

I turned to her and said, "I don't want us to get trapped here." I sped up and we made it through the crowd. I couldn't help but remember the peaceful crossing of buffalo in Oklahoma as this crowd frantically crisscrossed before us.

As we got closer to Dearing, we did not see any more rioting. In the house, I saw on the news that the National Guard was moving in. Being a military person myself, I personally felt a great sense of relief. Even if 1,000 Detroit cops were coming in, I would have been worried, because I believe the citizens would have been more agitated at the sight of them.

I was distressed, however, to hear that snipers were shooting at the National Guard. I found it ironic that I did not have on my uniform the day were almost trapped in the riot; I was in civilian clothes—would I have been in danger if I had been seen in my military uniform?

"I was distressed, however, to hear that snipers were shooting at the National Guard. . . I was in civilian clothes—would I have been in danger if I had been seen in my military uniform?"

I was very worried for my wife, since I had to leave in a week. What kind of city would she be left in? The greatest worry at the height of the riot for me was not knowing what was going to happen next: would the riot spread over the entire city?

Fortunately, the riot was over within five days, so I felt a little better when I had to leave. Unfortunately, when I later returned from Vietnam, I saw how much Detroit had changed.

RAYNE SHOWERS

The Riot Act

Our streets became congested with a disturbing cadence unfamiliar to a fairly quiet, working class neighborhood. We were a neighborhood under siege amidst gunshots, police and fire sirens, screeching car tires, overlapping low-flying helicopter whirrs and excited chatter, which bounced off the house from every direction. Like Dorothy in *The Wizard of Oz* swept up in a tornado, the events extended beyond the comprehension of a ten-year-old girl in the Motor City on a hot day in July.

Interrupted by the sound of popping noises outside like fireworks, mysterious and unrecognizable at first, the rhythmic gunfire forced my family and neighbors towards the sanctuary of our homes. Afraid, people walking through the neighborhood ran to the alcoves and doorways of nearby buildings.

Although my parents and maternal grandparents ushered us away from the windows, we—my little sister, cousin (who had come to spend the weekend) and I couldn't imagine what was happening. The phone rang repeatedly in the background, but Grandmother whispered to each caller, "We're okay." At that moment, the feared unknown was random shooting in the streets and from rooftops.

When their backs were turned, we peeked between the living room curtains: women and men ran back and forth between our home and the neighbors'. The people's arms overflowed with ladies, infant and children's clothing, shoeboxes, fresh vegetables and cases of canned goods.

People carried bakery boxes piled high from across the street. Men and women partnered to balance sofas and mattresses on their shoulders and backs. They used the property of others as an escape route for their bounty. Our house is on Lothrop Street between Dexter and Grand River Avenues, near West Grand Boulevard on the west side of Detroit. It is a bustling business artery set between three different streets with a mix of businesses and homes. Standing on my front porch facing Lothrop, to my left is Dexter that connects to West Grand Boulevard, and to my right, Grand River, which runs from downtown to the suburbs.

Across the street from my home is a building that holds the Charles Furniture Warehouse on the bottom and offices above. Facing the front of my house is State Representative John Conyers' office. Often, looking out of my upstairs bedroom window, I see him on the phone or talking with Rosa Parks while she takes notes or uses a typewriter. The phone rang again. Dad listened with a frown on his face, hung up and told us that men using soda pop bottles filled with gasoline and stuffed with pieces of rags were lighting and throwing them to start fires.

Suddenly, I heard Grandfather outside yell to a man across the street with a soda pop bottle in his hand. He ran across the street to speak with him. I went upstairs to my bedroom window to get a better look. Grandfather, hands gesturing seriously, explained something to the man with the bottle. Standing at the top of the stairway landing, I heard him describe to the family how he pleaded with the man not to set the building on fire with a Molotov cocktail.

The explosion shook the house. Grandfather rushed to the front porch, stuck his head back in the house and called for Dad to help him pull the water hose to the front and fill up pails of water. In a calm voice, Dad escorted me, my sister and cousin to the basement. Mom and Grandmother refused to leave them. Great-Grandmother was already in the basement, praying aloud. Dad ran up the basement steps and outside to join Grandfather while Mom and Grandmother watched from the living room. Before long, Grandmother came down to the basement to check on us. The phone rang.

After a few moments, we heard her scream, "Oh, no!" Grandmother mumbled something about her mother. Not knowing what to do, I called to Mom upstairs who came down hurriedly.

Grandmother couldn't compose herself and fell into my mom's arms while saying her sister called, and their mother was alright but something terrible happened. Someone set the gas station afire next to her mother's home. The powerful explosion skipped over her house but burned down all the other houses on her side of the street.

Leaving Great-Grandmother, Grandmother and Mom in the basement I ran upstairs to get Dad or Grandfather to help calm them all. My sister and cousin followed me up the stairs to the living room, but it was empty. We kneeled on the sofa, pulled the curtains back and were surprised to see an orange glow directly across the street. I heard Grandfather say angrily,

"Damn, I asked that punk not to throw that thing. Told him we had kids on this block."

Everything was on fire! The office, warehouse and all the stores were swallowed up in flames. Slowly, whitish gray smoke billowed from the sides of windows in Representative John Conyers' office, and sneaked through the cracks of the furniture warehouse door. Then, the building's windows began to burst and pieces of glass sprayed the area like a hail shower. Every man on the block was in front with a water hose, hosing down their homes to keep them cool from the fire's intensity. Neighbors banned together to help each other. It seemed like forever before fire trucks finally arrived, but by now it was too late. My whole world was ablaze.

The firemen fought the orange monster; the burning smell smothered those outside and began to penetrate indoors. For the remainder of the day, the battery of firemen wrestled with recurring fires across the street made difficult by furniture and mattresses stored in the warehouse. By the time daylight slipped away the flames were almost extinguished. Gray and white smoldering smoke replaced the bright orange and black burned palette. I stepped out onto the front porch, against my mother's wishes, to see the aftermath of the day. A loud rumbling vibrated the porch, making me think an earthquake was happening, but instead I looked up to see two army tanks rolling down the block. A few soldiers walked alongside, just like in a movie or on the TV news of Vietnam. One tank rolled to a stop, right in front of my house. Soldiers climbed out and then positioned themselves up and down the street. A few even sat on our front lawn.

Things were strangely quiet. Mom said that the TV newsman announced a curfew was in place, so no one could be on the streets at dark. We all gathered on the porch, huddled together and noticed our neighbors doing the same. The presence of soldiers gave me a strange feeling of safety. Their stern faces stared at us as though we were the enemy as we stared back at them.

Grandmother went into the kitchen and soon called my name. I found her in the kitchen making bologna and peanut butter and jelly sandwiches, and stirring an ice-filled pitcher of her much loved lemonade. I asked why she was making so many sandwiches and she said, “To feed the soldiers.”

After washing our hands, cousin and I helped her stack the sandwiches on one of her favorite entertaining platters and placed the drinks on a colorful tray. She called to Dad and Grandfather to help carry things outside. After passing out sandwiches and lemonade to Mom, Great-Grandmother, my sister and cousin sitting on the porch, Grandmother, Dad and Grandfather went down the front walkway with me tagging along. Grandmother asked the soldier who looked like he was in charge if they were hungry, and he said, “Yes.” We began to pass out sandwiches and glasses. The stern faces broke into small smiles. I heard a few of them say “Thank you, Ma’am,” and “This lemonade sure is good.”

While the soldiers took their positions for the night, one of the neighbors who owned a security guard company did the same; armed with his rifle he patrolled the alleyway most of the night and the corner store where his company provided security.

I tried to make sense of what happened that day. At ten years-old, nothing had prepared me for the moments that led to the destruction of my neighborhood. Nothing prepared me for hiding from sniper bullets. Ultimately, I tried to be brave in spite of the panic-stricken look in the eyes of the adults around me.

There was no way to know how much the world as I knew it had changed by the actions of others on that day but deep inside I felt that my innocence, my life between the Boulevard and the Avenues, would no longer be enough for whatever tomorrow would bring.

MARY MOCERI

I'm trying very hard to remember the Riots of '67 in Detroit. I remember that I was a mother of two and pregnant with my third child when we heard the news. Living in Roseville, we didn't see any fires or hear any shots, but I saw the National Guard jeeps and trucks with soldiers driving down our street.

We were all in awe, thinking the riots were going to get closer. Some people who had family living closer to the riot area went and picked them up to bring them home with them. My sister and mother lived on the east side of Detroit, but they were not scared of their neighborhood.

One way the authorities had to try to curb the mayhem going on was to limit the amount of gas you could buy and they would not sell you gas in a can. The neighbors would get together in the evening and talk about the day's events that we saw on TV. I remember that a lot of the guys had gone out and bought a gun—most of them never shot a gun and probably haven't shot it since, but it was for their protection. Or just in case the riot came to town.

"I remember that a lot of the guys had gone out and bought a gun—most of them never shot a gun and probably haven't shot it since, but it was for their protection. Or just in case the riot came to town."

After I looked back into my memory I looked up some statistics and what I found out was the riots lasted fromJuly 23rd to July 30th. Forty people died and over 2,000 were injured. Over 5,000 people were left homeless by rioting and burning in Detroit black neighborhood. It took 4,700 Field Paratroopers and 8,000 National Guardsmen to stop the destruction.

MONO D'ANGELO

1967 Detroit Riot

In 1967, I was employed as an apprentice draftsman in the American Motors Building located on Plymouth Road just east of Greenfield Road. I had been working there since graduating from high school, three years earlier. A family friend had arranged an interview for a job in the mailroom and I was hired almost immediately.

The building was headquarters for much of the company's executive offices, public relations, labor relations and product design and development activities. The facility was large and staffed primarily by white-collar employees. While the surrounding neighborhoods were racially integrated, the majority of employees were white and lived outside the city.

The mailroom operation was no different than the other departments. The staff was almost entirely white, except for one black male employee named Wesley. After receiving my work assignment, I quickly became acquainted with my new co-workers and began working alongside Wes, as he liked to be called.

He was a few years older than me and married. He had two young daughters, whose pictures he proudly displayed on his workbench. He was an easy person to like, worked hard and got along with all his managers and co-workers. He became my teacher and, ultimately, a friend.

Wes was taking engineering classes at night and often told me I should consider doing the same. He had recently been interviewed for a drafting position in engineering that could result in not only a good raise, but also the beginning of a whole new career. Even after his promotion came through, he continued to encourage me to follow suit whenever we spoke.

"This is good work and you can learn a skill that will make you a lot of money," he would say. He was right and I eventually followed him into the engineering group. I had no idea how right he was, as it was that job which led me into a lifelong career in automotive design engineering.

On that hot afternoon in July, I recall returning to work from lunch. The office air conditioning was a welcome relief from the summer's sticky humidity. Casual dress codes had not been invented yet and all engineering employees were required to wear white shirts and dark ties at all times, making the heat feel even more intolerable. It was an allmale workplace, and other than a few secretaries, there were no women on the engineering staff. The room was the size of a football field and housed hundreds of engineers and draftsmen, almost all of whom were white.

Radios were not allowed on during work hours, but could be used on lunch breaks. Arriving at my drawing board, I saw groups of men gathered together listening to news reports on the radio. I walked up to one of the groups and asked,

"What's going on?"

"There's some kind of civil disturbance on 12th Street and they're saying it's turning into a race riot," someone answered.

The concept of a race riot did not immediately resonate with me. While I had observed some racial bigotry among a few neighbors and acquaintances, I don't recall that prejudice affecting my behavior. I never considered myself overtly prejudiced, but what I didn't understand then, only to realized several years later, was that by living in my all white suburb, I too, participated in a form of racial segregation common in Detroit at the time. Still, the idea of wanting to hurt someone just because of his or her race was a disturbing fact and I wondered what would happen next. It didn't take long to find out.

A short time later, the department manager called an emergency meeting in the drafting room and announced,

"For those of you who have not heard the news, there is a large scale riot occurring in another part of the city. Reports in the media show the situation has grown worsethan expected and National Guard troops have been called in to help restore the peace. Our security people have been advised by Detroit police the situation is unpredictable, so anyone who would like to leave work can do so immediately."

The unprecedented management action to close the corporate headquarters only added to everyone's growing uneasiness. The exodus began as soon as the meeting was over and a somber parade of employees left the office in a quiet haste. As I walked down the main corridor toward the exit, I spotted Wes a short distance ahead of me. The hallway was crowded and I could not catch up to him. I don't knowwhat I would have said to him if I had. I can only imagine how conflicted he must have been feeling, being one of only a few black employees among the hundreds of white engineers.

The nearby corner bar, usually a crowded after work oasis, was locked up and dark. Security guards had been stationed in all areas of the complex. I saw no weapons, but many carried walkie-talkie radios and lengths of pipe. My sense of uncertainty grew as I climbed into my car and exited the parking lot. Neighborhood shortcuts I often took without thinking now came into question. I drove west on Plymouth Road straight toward the Southfield Expressway, avoiding any side streets. I recall the eerie, silent landscape of what was usually, a busy local shopping district. The entire area now lay still and deserted. Once I was in the "trench," as the Southfield Expressway was often called, I felt a strange sense of relief, as if I had somehow escaped the madness.

Like most suburban Detroiters, I watched the unfolding drama of the following two days on television. I recall being stunned at the level of the violence and to what means the authorities resorted to in order to put down the riot. The nightly scenes of violence and devastation being broadcast by local television stations resembled the news film clips coming from the war in Viet Nam.

I had lived a large part of my life in Detroit, near Mack and Van Dyke. I went to school there with black classmates, but I really never gave racial differences much thought. In retrospect, I think I was very naïve and even oblivious, to the racial tensions of that time, perhaps because I had never been directly affected. But watching U.S. paratroopers engage in running gun battles with the black citizens of my city certainly was a shocking dose of racial reality.

I called my supervisor each morning to determine if I should return to work. There was no answer for two days but after the violence had subsided, I decided to report for work. The drive north on the Southfield Expressway was noticeably less congested. I exited onto Plymouth Road and proceeded east toward the American Motors Building. I saw no evidence of any trouble in the area. The neighborhood around the AMC building also seemed unscathed. Arriving at the employee's parking lot, I noticed plant security personnel stopping each vehicle entering the facility.

"Your supervisor's name, please," they asked. The name I provided was crosschecked against a master list and I was allowed to enter.

I parked in my usual spot and noticed the lot was filling up as usual. That was a comforting feeling, as if things would somehow return to normal, whatever that might be. Moments later, I saw Wes enter the lot. He parked a few spaces away from me, so I waited for him. I found myself becoming anxious about what we would say to one another, as if we were somehow combatants in this awful experience that had just occurred.

He saw me waiting for him, and he waved. I could see a slight smile on his face and that made me feel a little better.

"Morning," he said.

"Hi, Wes. How are you doing? Everything okay?"

"Yeah. None of that bad stuff happened near me, but the wife and kids were a little scared."

I felt relieved that the violence had not reached him and that maybe the riot and all its racial implications could be put behind us. I was wrong.

As we approached the building entrance, there were several white janitors smoking in a nearby alcove. It was unusual to see anyone there at that time of the morning and I think Wes glanced at them out of nothing more than innocent curiosity. One of the janitors noticed Wesley's attention and shouted,

"What are you lookin' at, boy?" Up until that moment, I had been a distant spectator to the riot's tragic events of the previous two days, but the janitor's epithet instantly changed that.

Wes stopped and glared at them. I'd never seen him mad at anyone, but he was clearly upset. His smile vanished, his jaw tightened and furrows of anger appeared on his brow. It was obvious the janitors were looking for a confrontation so I grabbed Wesley's arm and said,

"Forget it, man. They're just jealous assholes looking to start something. They ain't worth your time or trouble."

Wes stood motionless for a few moments and continued to stare at the men in the alcove. There was no way to tell what he was going to do, and if the scene turned ugly, I distinctly remember wondering what I would do. Time seemed to stand still for the next thirty seconds. Fortunately, Wes had the courage and foresight to walk away from what could have been a career-threatening incident.

I felt relieved that the violence had not reached him and that maybe the riot and all its racial implications could be put behind us. I was wrong.

I was not aware of any further such comments directed at Wes at any time following the riot. As I think back, I attribute that to the fact that he was a decent man and everyone one who knew him respected that. Business in the Engineering group resumed its normal routine.

I left the company a couple of years later to accept ajob with Ford. The design engineering business was a small community then, where engineers and designers often moved to new jobs only to rejoin former coworkers again.

Over the years, I kept in touch with some of my AMC coworkers and had heard Wesley went on to a successful engineering career there, eventually moving into a management role.

I often wonder what might have been had he pushed the racial slur by the bigoted janitor into a full confrontation. I've not talked to

Wes since I left American Motors, but whenever the subject of the 1967 riot comes up, I still feel good thinking that my small part in preventing that morning confrontation may have enabled Wesley to enjoy the success he had worked so hard to achieve.

DARRYLE BUCHANAN

A Childhood Shattered: My Memories of the 1967 Rebellion in Detroit

Before we moved to Virginia Park, I barely noticed anything beyond my friendships. I grew up surrounded by Filipino, Chaldean, and white kids. We visited each other's homes and played together, and I didn't see much difference for a long time. But when we moved to Virginia Park, everything changed. The harsh realities of life hit me in a way I wasn't prepared for. It wasn't that the new environment was terrible—it was just *different.*

Suddenly, I found myself in a densely populated community. My father's parents owned a two-family apartment, and right next to us was an apartment building. It was like that all along the street—multi-unit homes, four-flat buildings, small apartments, and large apartments. The number of people was overwhelming, especially coming from quieter neighborhoods like Conant Gardens and Highland Park. But it was also exciting. There were so many kids to play with and get into trouble with. There was always something going on.

But then, that was also when I first noticed poverty. Growing up, I hadn't seen people struggle financially. Suddenly, it was all around me. Some of my new friends had parents who barely got by. It wasn't like I felt separate from them — it was just something I noticed. We were all friends, with no distinction, but it changed how I saw the world.

Then there was the police. Before moving to Virginia Park, I had barely seen a police car. Now, their presence was constant, and their flashing lights were a regular sight. My first encounter with them happened when I was around nine or ten years old. A few of us had found a pack of cigarettes and were running around trying to find matches to light them. We were playing in the alley when the cops rolled up. "What are you boys doing?" they yelled before chasing us for trying to smoke. I couldn't understand it. Why was all this over a few cigarettes? I was scared, but I didn't see the big deal. Couldn't they have just taken them from us and told us to go home?

Things quickly escalated in that neighborhood. I wasn't even 12, but I was starting to realize that life here was different. My mom warned me about Twelfth Street, saying, "Stay off it." But the more she told me to stay away, the more I was drawn to it. I had to walk on it anyway when I went to St. Agnes, my school. The first time I walked down Twelfth Street, I was amazed. It was *alive*. There were stores, theaters, restaurants—it was a bustling, self-contained world. Everything you needed was right there. On our block alone, we had a pharmacy, a barbershop, a hardware store, a lounge, a market, and even a dairy. As a kid, I thought it was paradise.

But beneath that energy, tensions were building up.

Then came that momentous morning in July. I was an altar boy at St. Agnes and had woken up early to prepare for the 8 a.m. Mass. I could hear people outside and thought, *Wow, they're partying early today.* I even smelled smoke and thought someone was barbecuing. But when my mom called and told me not to go to church and that something was happening on Twelfth Street, I stepped onto our porch. The street was alive but in a different way. People were moving up and down, confused and agitated. The looting hadn't started yet, but it was only a matter of time.

I'll never forget my mom coming home that day in a police car. Usually, she took the bus to work at Henry Ford Hospital, but everything was different that morning. My mind was racing as I stood on the porch, watching her step out of the car. I'd seen too many cops in our neighborhood. I'd heard too many stories. And now, my mom was in a police car — it made me worry about how people would see us.

It was a strange time. My friends and I sneaked over to Twelfth Street to see what was happening. The streets were packed with people—so many, and all angry. I understood why. We had been living under constant police surveillance, feeling the weight of their eyes on us. My early run-ins with them, like being chased for smoking cigarettes, were minor compared to what older boys had to face. I saw guys who used to be the coolest in the neighborhood—those who wore their crisscross sweaters and mohair slacks—come back from Vietnam, broken. They weren't the same. And they were angry too.

Twelfth Street, once lively, was becoming unrecognizable. I watched buildings burn, felt the chilling rush of when a structure collapsed, and even saw rats scurry out of the flames. The smell of burning wood and plastic hung in the air like a heavy, inescapable blanket. And the sirens—they never ceased. It was a constant, mournful wail, as if the city itself was crying.

I spent most of those days on our porch, watching the world unfold. The National Guard and federal troops moved into our neighborhood, enforcing martial law. There were curfews, lights out at night, and tanks rumbling down the streets. One night, I saw my mom leave for work again, this time in an unmarked black car. It sped down Virginia Park with no lights on, as if trying to hide from the chaos around it.

I kept going back to Twelfth Street, even though it got smaller each time. I remember watching Dr. Maben's Pharmacy being looted. He was a Black man, a pillar of the community, and I stood there pleading with people not to destroy his business. But the chaos had taken over. It didn't matter that it was a Black-owned business—everything fueled the madness. Looking back, I realize they were after the drugs.

As the rebellion continued, I felt a strange mix of fear and understanding. I had grown up with police harassment. I had seen friends beaten, humiliated, and treated like criminals. I had learned the rules of survival from older boys and the Black Panthers—how to talk to the police, how to stand, and how to make yourself seem small and unthreatening. But now, it was about more than just survival. It was about something more significant. This wasn't a riot, not in the way people typically think of riots. This was a rebellion against a system that had kept us down for so long.

In the aftermath, nothing was the same. Once so vibrant, Twelfth Street was a shell of its former self. The sirens had stopped, but the damage was already done. The city had changed forever, and so had I.

WALTER CAMPBELL

The summer of the 1967 Detroit Riot was a long and hot one. There was a lot of hopelessness and despair, with many people out of work, people sitting around with nothing to do and no money. The riot almost seemed destined to happen.

On top of this, the police gave black people a hard time. The "Big Four," the "elite" police squad, cruised the streets. They wore long leather coats in the winter and would beat the hell out of you. I called them the "Gestapo."

During the riots, the police stopped me and two friends of mine, Carl and Glenn, at an intersection. We were in Detroit's Northend, at the Chrysler Freeway and Holbrook. We were on our way to work as switchboard operators for the City; we also typed work orders for repairs on buildings around the city. Our work building was known as the Central Building Maintenance on Russell and Erskine (which I believe are now lofts). With the riots going on, people could not go too far from home. But, like many people who still had jobs, we had to get to work.

Along with the police, the National Guard was there, for I distinctly remember them all being in two types of uniforms. They had their guns out, and I could not help but think that here we were in broad daylight, and they had live bullets. One could sense from them a sort of white supremacy mindset, that our black lives had little meaning.

I had heard that the National Guard had shot up apartment buildings on 12th Street with gunfire from tanks. They let us go on to work, eventually.

ELDER MINOR PALM, JR.

The Riot of 1943: Trouble on the Homefront

After sixty-three years, I still can remember the riot of 1943. On February 5, 2006, God blessed me to turn 80-years-old. In 1943, I was a teenage boy of only 17 years.

At that time, I was attending Northwestern High School on Detroit's west side. I had a part-time job after school working at one of the chain stores of Cunningham's drugstores located on Grand River at Oakman Boulevard. At this time, white people lived in this area.

After school, I rode the streetcar to the store and back home. The manager of this store was Russian. He was friendly. There was a white lady over the lunch counter in the store. She appreciated me and showed much appreciation to me for doing the cleaning when she called for me to come and do it.

My job was called a "portor"; I washed the outside of those big windows. I had to wash and scrape off the sheets of advertisement paper glued on the windows. Then I put up the new ads. I brought up items from the stock or storage room. I swept the floors and mopped them, too.

When I got home, I did my homework and ate dinner my dear mother fixed for our family of six. I am the only son and oldest child of four children born to my loving parents, Elder and Missionary Minor Palm, Sr. We had a very close family.

Late one Sunday evening in 1943, the news on our large tabletop wooden radio told about trouble out on Belle Isle Park. A story was told about a white man who had abused a black woman. As the evening grew on, the news got more serious. A lot of people, both black and white, got involved in a massive and brutal fight. There was a lot of ugly namecalling going on. It got so bad that many police were called to try and control the raging trouble on Belle Isle.

The next day, on Monday, the violence and trouble had spread through the city of Detroit. There was a huge riot. The mayor, who was Mayor Jeffries, announced that there was going to be a curfew made. He said that no blacks could be on the street after six o'clock in the evening. The only ones who could be out were those going or coming from work. Otherwise, any other black people out would be arrested.

Soon, some state and national officials called for soldiers to camp out on Northwestern High School's field on Grand River near McGraw. Yes, right at my high school. The soldiers were armed and drove around Detroit in caravans night and day. The city was filled with them.

However, there were some rumors that some black gangsters drove in from Chicago to Detroit to help out the blacks in the riot. This made everything more explosive. My father worked at Ford Rouge Car Factory in Dearborn, Michigan. He was about 45-years-old at the time.

"Soon, some state and national officials called for soldiers to camp out on Northwestern High School's field on Grand River near McGraw. Yes, right at my high school."

The war, World War II, was going on. The United States government didn't want men to miss work. So, here in Detroit with the riot and curfew on, my father and other men tried to go on to work. Sometimes, the police would stop them to question them. My father was always a hardworking man. So he went on out into these dangerous conditions.

After about a week, the riot was over. When it ended, I went back to work at Cunningham's. There was a change of employees at the store. Before the riot, there were no black young ladies working in the drugstore. However, after the riot, there were black young ladies working there. I continued working there for a while, but later I got a job paying more money.

ELDER MINOR PALM, JR.

The Riot of 1967: "Burn, Baby! Burn!"

In the late 60's, there were great changes taking place in DetroitPlans were being made by leading blacks and whites to improve the city of Detroit for the black population. Congressman Charles C. Diggs made several trips back and forth from Washington, D.C. to Detroit.

The black population was moving from the west side to the northwest side. A great percentage of the Jewish population moved further west. They crossed Livernois towards Wyoming, then in within a few years, towards the Schaefer Road area. During this tremendous transitional time, Dexter Avenue, 12th Street and Linwood Avenue became heavily populated with blacks.

The black communities flourished with many businesses like barbershops, beauty shops, furniture stores, restaurants, markets, clothing stores, shoe shops, meat and fish markets, insurance companies, five-and-dime stores and other businesses. Neighborhoods were united. Homeowners took great pride in their property, schools, and community.

When it looked like blacks were going to go as far as they wanted and dreamed, Rap Brown and Stokely Carmichael made a move to reconstruct the old west side of Detroit. This brought on a great change in the city. Detroit was never the same.

On one Sunday evening, fires broke out on 12th Street, Lawton, Dexter, Warren and other major streets around Detroit. Many businesses were ravished and burned. The smell and sights of thick black smoke filled the air on those hot summer days.

My wife, Willie Lee, asked me to drive her around town to see what happened. Our three teenage children, Wanda, Rodger and Regina, went along with us. I drove on Warren where we saw stores being looted, ravished and burned out. Arabs who owned stores sat in chairs on sidewalks outside their stores with rifles across their laps.

We went down Dexter Avenue. There was Rap Brown on top of a theater with a loudspeaker in his hand. He was shouting, "Burn, Baby! Burn!" This urged the crowd of people on the streets to loot and do other unbelievable things. It kept the fire trucks roaring down our burning streets.

I drove down Linwood and Lawton. We passed a market with gigantic flames of bright orange fire. The flames burst through the stores and poured out toward the street as I slowly drove past. You could feel the intense hot fiery heat. Fires were erupting everywhere.

"The riot, fires and looting did something to strip everything bare in Detroit."

When we returned home that night, you could hear guns of all kinds shooting. Gun shooting went on all night. It sounded like a war zone with the tap-tap-tap and bangbang.

The riot, fires and looting did something to strip everything bare in Detroit. My wife and I had our winter clothes in a cleaners in the city. Our clothes were stored there until winter. We lost all of our winter clothing of suits, coats and other things because of the riot.

After the riot was all over, there were no stores nearby to buy food, meats, vegetables and other needed things. You couldn't shop in Detroit. People had to drive to Dearborn, Michigan to purchase mostly everything.

DOROTHY JACKSON KIMBLE

"The Catalyst" from A Mighty Long Way: A Memoir

Going north from Cameron, you eventually come upon the small city of Highland Park. Farther east, past Cameron but only half a block away, is the Chrysler Freeway; a little farther east is the city of Hamtramck. Going west from where we lived, the intersection of Twelfth Street (now known as Rosa Parks Boulevard) and Clairmount was about fifteen city blocks from our house. This is the famous intersection where the 1967 Detroit Riot began.

I remember the first day of the riot. It was on July 23, 1967. I leisurely awoke to a bright, hot Sunday morning around seven. Sam and the girls were still asleep. As I got out of bed and opened the blinds, I was unpleasantly surprised to see vast clouds of eerie, black smoke billowing in the sky at a distance towards the west. I tugged on Sam's arm to wake him up.

"Get up," I hollered, "I don't know where it's at—but there's something on fire!"

Sam jumped up and looked out the window. He said, "Something's on fire all right! Looks like it's up there around Twelfth Street and Clairmount." He quickly put on some clothes and went to find out from the neighbors what had happened. In a few minutes he came back excited and said:

"Dot, don't get all upset—I think they're rioting like they did in '43! Just stay in the house until I find out something else about what's going on." The neighborhood was already buzzing with rumors of how many people had been killed.

It was years later, in fact fairly recently, when I discovered that Laverne and Wanda, both just under twenty-one, had been out that

Saturday night—way past their curfew. They got caught up in the beginning of the riot while dropping their cousin Harvey home. Harvey lived west, just one block from the chaos that Laverne and Wanda had to travel through to get back home.

Laverne recalled the early hours of the riot:

"Harvey, Wanda, and myself had been out partying all night. Around 4:00 or 5:00 a.m. we dropped Harvey off at home on Clairmount and Fourteenth. As we crossed 12th Street we saw people breaking out store windows, looting the stores, and running through the streets carrying stolen goods and screaming. Stores were burning everywhere. There seemed to be mass hysteria."

Wanda also remembered what happened:

"I heard [store] burglar alarms going off. People had been out partying and a lot of them were high. They were breaking plate glass windows. We stopped the car and walked down the first block off Clairmount asking people what was going on. Some said they were mad because black people had been mistreated. They were saying things like, 'We're always the last to get hired and the first to get fired.' We went into a drugstore where people were taking merchandise and I decided to join in on the action. I grabbed some deodorant. The cops hadn't come yet, but we thought it was time to get out of there."

Laverne said:

"I knew the situation was extremely dangerous. I maneuvered the car through the crowds and 'put my foot to the metal.' We had to get home in one piece."

Twelfth Street from West Grand Boulevard to Clairmount was a crowded, gaudy, commercial street. In the wee hours of the Twenty-Third, during the heat of the night, a blind pig (a place where alcoholic beverages are sold illegally) located in that part of the city had been raided by the Detroit police. The news traveled quickly with rumors that white policemen were brutalizing black people. As the rumors spread, the exaggerations kindled volatile anger. The anger mixed with the hot weather. It was like a bomb had exploded; the area was in chaos. There were shootings and some of Detroit's citizens were killed. The blind pig incident touched off four anxiety-laden days of looting, burning, and sniping.

But there was an order to the disorder. Although looting and burning started in the Twelfth Street/Clairmount area, there were men who, mostly on Sunday and Monday, instigated thousands of people citywide into looting by breaking out plate glass windows of city stores, which were mostly pawnshops, furniture and grocery stores. The instigators moved from store to store making it easy for the men, women, and children who wanted to enter a store to loot it. When the looters finished getting what they wanted someone would come and set it on fire. The arsonists showed a definite preference for white-operated business establishments. A number of black-owned businesses were burned only because fires that started elsewhere had spread.

Our black dentist moved from Joy and Dexter to Puritan and Wyoming because the building where his office was located upstairs over a store had burned down.

When I first saw those eerie black clouds, they were in the distance. The ominous fires came much closer to home before that long stress filled day was over. Most of the white storekeepers in our immediate neighborhood, whose businesses were looted and burned, had been there for years.

As a teenager, Sam had liked working as a stock boy for Phil and his wife Lillie who were Jews. They owned "The Supermarket," one of the stores on Oakland that was burned down only a block away from where we lived.

The looters walked or rode in cars. They carried merchandise from the stores to their homes and merrily showed off what they had stolen. I was angry and afraid the arsonists might decide to set the houses on fire. The looters and arsonists I watched were people who lived in my neighborhood. I was disappointed and sad when I saw them greedily taking part in the looting. I didn't want any of the stolen goods brought into our house because I thought it would bring bad luck. I felt hurt when some of the close neighbors and friends that I had grown up with called me a "square." Law enforcement wasn't controlling the emergency and I felt helpless, but there was nothing I could do. Our neighborhood became "a war zone."

Sam didn't share my disappointment in our neighbors. He thought differently about the rioting. And in spite of my apprehension, he bought a pair of black leather dress shoes from one of the young men. He also bought a dark green, "sharkskin" summer suit. Sam still brings those shoes out of the closet every now and then and wears them for a day.

And for a long time he would periodically exercise to flatten his stomach muscles and shed a few pounds so he could bring out the suit and wear it. He'd tell me, "Look, Dot, I can still get in it." He looked good in his suit, too. But when Charisse, our oldest granddaughter, was sixteen, the suit had come into style for young girls to wear. Sam let her borrow it to wear to a party once and we haven't seen it since. I finally got over my distress concerning the clothes that Sam bought, but it took me a long time to do so.

Sam already knew how it felt to be in a war. He served in World War II in the Pacific Theater (a place of significant events) as a T5 (Technician Corporal) on the island of Okinawa and in Hawaii. He was in charge of the supplies (clothing, tools, artillery, etc.) for his platoon. Having tasted of war, he wasn't frustrated like I was during the riot. I had never been immersed in violence except for the times when my mother and stepfather's arguments became physical and I would be afraid he would hurt her.

In the 1943 Detroit Riot, when I was fourteen, the city erupted over an incident that was alleged to have occurred on Belle Isle. An article in The Detroit News dated in 1943 (I don't have the complete date) says, "Police stated the serious rioting started at the Forest Club." The club had a two-level roller-skating rink, a 107-foot bar and a 26-lane bowling alley. Sonnie Wilson was the black owner of the business that was located at Forest and Hastings streets.

The article further stated, "A crowd was incited by a false statement that a Negro woman and her baby had been hurled from the Belle Isle Bridge." The immensity of the 1943 riot didn't affect me like the 1967 riot did twenty-four years later. The ominous wailing of the civil disturbance sirens reminded me of the sirens I'd heard during World War II. The fires raging one city block from where I lived were frightening. The radio commentators drearily broadcast the latest reports all day long. There was apprehension among my neighbors and my children. All of this caused me to have stress.

At the time of the 1967 riot, the girls were ages twenty, nineteen, fourteen, and twelve. President Lyndon B. Johnson sent the National Guard into Detroit because of the civil disturbance. I don't know what fort or state they came from. One evening at dusk while the city was still in turmoil, a young white National Guardsman crept into our backyard holding his high-powered rifle with the attached bayonet pointed forward and up. We had three upstairs bedrooms, two on the front and one in the back of the house. Sam was asleep in our front bedroom. The girls and I had been in the back bedroom peeping out of the window when the trooper came into our yard. I quietly guided them along the floor to the top of the stairs where we crawled down to the reception hall, through the living room and on into the dining room going directly to the window facing the backyard. I could see well enough to know he was afraid. I was fearful that if he heard movement in our house his fear would cause him to shoot one of us. Silently I led my children back upstairs by crawling along the floor to the stairway. I will never forget the sight of that frightened young man, away from home, doing his duty patrolling the alleys and backyards of people who were just as fearful as he was.

Teresa remembers what happened the day after the National Guardsman entered our backyard:

"Me, Sylvia, and Grace and Carol (our neighborhood friends who were also sisters), were on the front porch talking when we all saw a green army tank drive slowly past on Oakland. Our house was situated so that we could look straight up Hague to Oakland, just a block away. In our panic, we scattered. I remember jumping off the first or second step from the porch and hitting the sidewalk. I skinned my left knee and have scars there as my memory. All of us ran towards the backyard to get out of sight."

A few months after the riot, people were still angry, sullen, and scared. One day I went to a business meeting in the suburbs with white friends from AA. When I realized it was getting dark and that I had to drive home alone, I became panicky. I had a fearful drive until I got close to home.

There was one joyful time that came after the riot. Charisse Laverne, our first grandchild, was born December 22, 1967 at Florence Crittenton Hospital in Detroit. She was our special Christmas gift that year.

In 1968, the year following the riot, our house was broken into several times while Sam, Laverne, Wanda and I were at work, and Sylvia and Teresa were in school. Since Sylvia was the first one home everyday during this time, she was the first to encounter the house in shambles. She remembered "inspecting" the house to see what was missing.

Sylvia called me at Maybee Elementary School, where I worked as a secretary, to tell me what had happened. Maybee was only six blocks from our house. I called the police and quickly left the school. Whoever broke in forced open the side door (that led to the kitchen or basement). The thieves took what they could find that could be quickly exchanged for money. We didn't have any proof of who did it but we had our suspicions. Whoever it was broke in a second time, not too soon after the first break-in.

One afternoon after the break-ins, I got in our car (a black 1964 Dodge Dart with red leather upholstery) and drove down Cameron. As I approached the corner at Wellington, there were three young men standing by another car parked at the curb. As I drove past, I recognized one of the men we suspected of breaking into our home. Strong resentment welled up in me and I had an almost overpowering urge to hit all of them with the car because I
thought all of them had something to do with the break-ins. But instead of hitting them, I glared at them as I drove past.

Another day I took our handgun out to the back porch and practiced my aim by shooting at a large thermometer that was hanging on the front of the garage. I was trying to send a message to the thieves: I HAVE A GUN THAT I WILL USE – AND I CAN HIT MY TARGET FAIRLY ACCURATELY!

Our neighborhood had become infested with drugs and the crime that goes along with it. The sound of gunfire close to the house was commonplace. I became anxious for my family and myself. I felt we needed to get away from the violence. The break-ins were the catalyst that caused Sam and I to move from our old house and neighborhood—where we had spent our childhood, teen years, and early adulthood—to another side of town about eleven miles northwest.

The time had come to begin again.

ABOUT THE WRITERS

Annmarie Thomas was born in Detroit, Michigan to Mr. and Mrs. Fred Thomas. She attended Northwestern High School and continued her education, graduating from Wayne County Community College and Eastern Michigan University as an English major. Ms. Thomas was employed with the University of Michigan as a Research Administrative Assistant in the Rheumatology Division. Her writing talents began when she was ten-years-old. She began writing poems using words from her imagination as a young child. Ms. Thomas was a member of the Detroit Writer's Guild from 1997-1999.

Sylvia McClain was a longtime writer for magazines and newspapers. She is the author of two books. One is a memoir, *Skipping Through Life: The Reason I Am* and the other a writer reference book, *The Write Life: A Beginning Writer's Guide to Writing, Money Management, Publishing & Marketing.* You can read writings by her in other anthologies such as the Chicken Soup® series and Gumbo for the Soul® books.

Wanda Kimble Keys was born and raised in Detroit, Michigan. She grew up in a neighborhood called the Northend. She graduated from Northern Senior High School and holds a B.A. from Wayne State University. Wanda has two children, Charisse and Darrick, and three grandchildren, James, Breonna and Dannaria. Wanda currently lives in Belleville, Michigan with her husband, Franklin. Wanda enjoys reading, African American reading groups, old movies, traveling and walking.

Brenda Cornish is a graduate of Wayne State University. She is a playwright.

Ronald Buchanan is retired from the United States Postal Service. A husband, father of three and grandfather, he was a drummer with the Sweet Beat Jazz Institute and studied under the late great Charlie Bannister of the Detroit Drum School. Ronald is also a collector of jazz albums.

Walter Campbell is a retired postal carrier for the United States Postal Service Fenkell Station. Before that, he worked for the City of Detroit. An avid athlete, he won several trophies in league softball and participates in bowling leagues with his wife, Brenda. Walter is the father of four, a grandfather of five, and a beloved uncle.

As a ten-year-old during the 1967 Detroit Riot, **Rayne Showers** never forgot how she survived the experience and dealt with the aftermath that stuck with her into adulthood, always bubbling beneath the surface to be told from a youthful perspective. From her first stab at creative writing in 7th grade Catholicism class where she tried to employ ancient Haiku poetry techniques to describe heavenly matters, her major writing influence—her mother—offered the budding writer's services to help write the obituaries of family and friends. Rayne has always been aware of her yearning to engage others with storytelling whether through prose, business plans or website content. Her work is a combination of multiple passions: storytelling, writing and music, three things deeply rooted in the history of the place known as the Motor City.

Elder Minor Palm, Jr. is a songwriter of many gospel songs. His first story, "Joe Louis Taught Me to Read," was published by the Detroit Writer's Guild in their anthology.

Mono D'Angelo is a novelist, poet, visual artist and freelance writer. He was the President of the Poetry Society of Michigan and director of Downriver Poets and Playwrights, a literary critique group. His publishing credits include his novel, *Powers of Fate,* numerous poetry anthologies as well as many online short story publications. He has contributed freelance articles to the *Detroit News, Detroit Free Press,* Heritage Newspapers, and *Trips & Journeys Travel Magazine.*

The late **Mary Moceri**'s essay was submitted by her loving grandchildren, Brent Moceri, and his sister, Toni.

Dorothy Jackson Kimble was a retired Detroit Public Schools secretary. She lived in Detroit with her husband of 59 years, Sam Kimble. In 1996 she joined The Detroit Black Writer's Guild (aka Detroit Writer's Guild), a local organization. The Guild published "Rabbi," a short story written by Dorothy, in their 1996 publication, *Day's Dawn* and "When Mom Paid Taxes Streetcar Trip Was Daughter's Fun" in *Paradise Valley Days* in 1998. Dorothy also published a family history, *Bloodline*, in 1999.

Darryle Buchanan is a tireless advocate for youth and community development. He is the former Director of The Obama Foundation's, My Brother's Keeper Initiative for the state of Michigan. He proudly served as President of the Southfield Board of Education, of which he was a trustee from 2005 – 2014. He diligently serves as a mentor for students who are in the greatest need of compassion and understanding and he has been instrumental in involving fellow members of the community in this endeavor. He co-founded a non-profit organization, Transition Basketball of Michigan, using players' love of athletics to inspire them to achieve success in other areas of their lives. As a result of participating in this program, many young men have received athletic and academic scholarships, networked with business and community leaders, and have been motivated to attain higher levels of academic and personal accomplishment. He has also served as vice president of the Michigan Association of School Boards' Board of Directors (MASB). Currently Mr. Buchanan serves as boys varsity head basketball coach at Southfield Arts & Technology High School. Born and raised in Detroit, Michigan, he is a proud graduate of St. Martin de Porres High School and completed his undergraduate studies at Wayne State University He is married to his wife of 34 years and they are the parents of two college educated adult sons.

Editorial Staff

Heather Buchanan, Editor-in-Chief, is an award-winning publisher and producer. She is the creator of many projects, including *Creation Beliefs* an exhibit for the Charles H. Wright Museum of African American History. Buchanan is a past winner of the MetroTimes' "Best Of: Literary" category. Buchanan's work appears in a variety of anthologies, including Daimler-Chrysler's *The Spirit in the Words.* A past Poet-in-Residence for the Detroit Public Library system, she has also served as Fiction Writer-in-Residence at the Westland Public Library and was a Master Fiction writer in the YMCA New York Program. Buchanan teaches workshops across the country. A two-time national fellow, Ms. Buchanan is the owner of Aquarius Press, a national press. A past COO of the Wayne County Council for Arts, History & Humanities, she was also the VP of the Great Lakes Independent Publishing Association (GLIPA). Buchanan is the author of *Victors: A Novel of Love, War and Jazz,* based on the true story of the Harlem Hellfighters of World War I.

Sharon Stanford was a Senior Editor for Aquarius Press. The former President of the Detroit Writer's Guild, Sharon has worked as a feature writer for the *Michigan Chronicle* with her articles appearing in Michigan and Canada. In 2000, Sharon won the Grand Prize in the Gertrude Johnson Williams Literary Contest for Ebony Magazine for her short story, "Fannie Lou's Dream." Her short stories have been published in Chicken Soup for the Soul® and *On the Shores of Detroit.* She has also worked as an editor for Chicken Soup for the Soul®.

Dr. Debraha Watson was the Interim Vice-Chancellor for Educational Affairs for Wayne County Community College. She is currently working on a literary collection.

Regeania Hunter is an English instructor and worked for Delphi Corporation. She also manages a theatrical production company with her brother.

Teresa "Teki" Kimble has been published thrice by the Detroit

Writer's Guild: "The Revival" in *Day's Dawn: A Short Story Anthology* (1996) and "Teki's Carrot Cake" in *Food for the Spirit: A Black History Cookbook* (1999). She received Honorable Mention from the Guild in 2000 for "Negro League Romance," which was published in a chapbook, and is a novella in progress. Teki (pronounced tea key) is a former book reviewer and freelancer for *CityView newspaper* where she interviewed local authors Lee Meadows (*Silent Conspiracy*) and Richard Goree (*Goree Island*). She was Chief Editor of *A Mighty Long Way: A Memoir (2004) by Dorothy Jackson Kimble,* a Detroit bestseller. When time is available she creates and tries hard to complete the numerous short stories she's written over the years.

About the Living Detroit Book Series

Pledged to preserve the history of the city of Detroit and the memories of its residents, Aquarius Press introduces the Living Detroit Book Series, found in your local bookstores and Amazon.com.

www.ingramcontent.com/pod-product-compliance
Lightning Source LLC
Chambersburg PA
CBHW020534120726
47904CB00003B/1075

9780971821484